MW00939441

What To Do In…Puerto Vallarta, Jalisco, Mexico

Volume 8

Copyright © 2015 by CC Thomas

All rights reserved. This book or any parts thereof may not be reproduced in any form without written permission. Printed in the United States of America.

Published by CC Thomas Writing Solutions, LLC.
Indiana, USA.
www.iknowfuntravels.blogspot.com
www.ccthomaswriter.com

Library of Congress Cataloging-in-Publication Date

Thomas, CC
    What To Do In…Puerto Vallarta, Jalisco, Mexico. Volume 8/CC Thomas.

978-1508418726 (pbk. alk. 5x8 Paper)

1.   Travels—Mexico. 2. Travels-Jalisco, Mexico. 3. Travels-Puerto Vallarta, Jalisco, Mexico.

All the pathos and irony of leaving one's youth behind is thus implicit in every joyous moment of travel: one knows that the first joy can never be recovered and the wise traveler learns not to repeat successes, but tries new places all the time. – Paul Fussell

Dedication

This series of books is dedicated to Martha C. Thomas, a traveler of immense imagination and purpose. It is to her that I owe my unquenchable wanderlust.

The world is a better place for her having trod upon it.

Table of Contents

On and Off the Beaten Path

One of my favorite scenes in a movie comes from a cartoon. It is from the Disney classic *Cars*. In it, the main character, Lightning McQueen, is racing across the desert to California when he breaks down in Radiator Springs, an unknown and forgotten locale. McQueen is forced to stay in the town and learned that it used to be a famous hot-spot on Route 66, before the "Interstate" (the true villain of the movie and small towns everywhere) came along and ruined the flavor, the economy, and the life of the town.

How many of us are like McQueen? Racing down the interstates, intent only on our next destination? Perhaps we can all learn a lesson from that fallible cartoon car. Namely, don't be so focused on your destination that you don't pay attention to the journey.

On your next vacation, use these guides to help you find some spots mostly off the beaten path, spots that locals know, but are unknown to most tourists. These are activities and eateries that are well worth making the time and money for.

These guide books will give you some fun and economical places to visit. Many of them will be places you might have heard of, but I always try to visit the out of the way, and forgotten spots, too. The other half of the book will focus on places to eat. I will never give a review of a place that is nationally known. I will instead focus on "mom and pop" places, or little "dives", that most tourists would skip. My top focus is on delicious eats, but ambiance will come a close second. I will also include a bit of history and some fun trivia. Hopefully, you'll find all you need to have a trip of a lifetime. If you like this volume, check out my other titles with reviews for locations all over the world.

All books can be ordered through Amazon, either printed or on Kindle. Another option is to visit my website, www.ccthomaswriter.com, or my travel blog, www.iknowfuntravels.blogspot.com, where a different locale is featured bi-monthly. These shortened versions will hopefully whet your appetite to try the longer volumes, which gives more information and detail about each place listed.

Note: Please be advised that all information was current at time of publication. If you find that the information provided therein is incorrect, please contact the author at ccthomaswriter@gmail.com.

As with any adventure, it's always smart to be prepared. Take advantage of the phone numbers and websites provided in the travel guide to research before you go. It's also been my experience that most places are closed on Mondays, so be sure to call on those days. Happy Trails!

Introduction to the Area

When I tell people our next vacation will be to some location in Mexico, they invariably ask, "Is it safe?" I have to admit I have no idea where this strange idea that Mexico is full of crime and danger comes from. Sure, I've heard stories of Mexican cartels, but I hazard a guess that strolling down any street in downtown Los Angeles or New York or New Orleans would be just as risky. I have never once felt in danger. Everywhere you look, there are police cars and police stationed in tourist areas with machine guns. Me, I like having police with machine guns. If you don't feel safe with that, nothing will make you feel safe!

Regardless, tourism ranks as the top (legal) money-producing enterprise in Mexico, so tourists are treated like royalty. Jalisco is no exception. Almost everywhere you go, the locals speak English or a good smattering of English and Spanish. There are plenty of tour companies and restaurants that cater to visitors from other countries. Truthfully, I always feel a bit like a queen when visiting Mexico. They have cultivated a true sense of customer service and satisfaction that is missing in the United

States. Puerto Vallarta was even been named "Las Cuidad Más Amiable", or "The Friendliest City in the World" by Conde Nast in 2001. I would have to wholeheartedly agree.

Puerto Vallarta was one of the stops on the old TV show *The Love Boat*, for good

Endless sandy beaches, a warm sun, gentle lapping waves—what's not to love about Puerto Vallarta?

reason. It is beautiful and exotic and breath-taking. With an average daily temperature of 86 degrees, it is a year-round escape for people the world over. Puerto Vallarta is located on the Bahía de Banderas (Bay of Flags) on the Pacific Ocean and is a major tourist destination and a town rich in culture and history. A tropical paradise in a busy city would be the best way to describe it.

If all of that doesn't convince you, consider that Jalisco is the birthplace of tequila and it is the only place where tequila can be produced. Or, maybe the fact that numerous movies have been made there, or that it is fast becoming a top retirement destination for US and Canadian retirees will convince you. As a matter of fact, it has been called the "Best Place to Retire in the World" by the AARP (American Association of Retired Persons)!

Regardless of the many reasons, Puerto Vallarta needs to be at the top of any travel list.

Things to Do

You will never be at a loss for something to do in Puerto Vallarta. It includes endless beaches, a stunning mountain range, a quiet town, and a bustling city. In addition to being a friendly city and a great place to retire, it's also been named the "Best Holiday Destination in Mexico" by USNews.com, the "Most Romantic Place in Mexico" and "Favorite Beach Destination in Mexico" by About.com, as well as a "Top Ten Destination in Mexico" by Trip Advisor. There's plenty to do, and plenty of beautiful places to do nothing, but, if you do venture out, be sure to hit these amazing locations.

1. **Go By Sea: Snorkeling** at **Islas Marietas (Marietas Islands)**. This chain of islands is about one hour away from Puerto Vallarta and the boat trip alone is worth it. On the way, we saw scads of various sea birds, dolphins that practically jumped onto the deck of our boat, and an entire school of manta rays. In the winter months, the area is well-known for whale watching and I have no doubt it would be quite an adventure. We were fortunately there

during jellyfish hatching time, and seeing these tiny pink and clear creatures surrounding the boat was a fantasy that Walt Disney could only dream about. So beautiful! However, the truly unbelievable sight was the secluded beach at Marietas. To get to it, you have to snorkel through a water tube. It was rough swimming and seemed to take forever, but once you get inside, the trip is well worth it. The islands were once used by the Mexican government as target practice and the leftover damage is now a beach that is inside one of these

Swimming through the water tube to Islas Marietas is not for the faint at heart. The swim is rigorous—I'm glad I did it before I got too much older!

craters, completely surrounded and only accessible by water. There is also a small grotto inside that you can crawl

But, all that exertion was worth it to see the hidden beach and grotto.

to. From there, we went to **Los Arcos (The Arches)** that had the best snorkeling we have ever done--and we have snorkeled in most of the Caribbean! Jellyfish, octopus, 'Nemo' fish--the two hours felt like ten minutes. Plus, it's one of your few chances to see a Blue-footed Booby in the wild! We used the local company **Cruise Vallarta** on the *Vallarta Sol* and were given breakfast, lunch, a snack and an open bar. The staff were amazing and seemed to have a heart for

Snorkeling at Los Arcos was the best I've ever done. Scads of fish and other wildlife were everywhere.

conservation. There are only a couple of touring companies even allowed to do this tour, so plan far in advance. This cruise company will pick you up on the local pier and deliver you right back to the taxi area. So convenient! Phone is (011-052-322)225-4679. If you're using your cell phone, call 044-322-306-0239. For more information, check the website

at
www.mexonline.com/cruisevallarta.htm.

2. **Go By Land: Four-wheeling** the
   Sierra Madre Mountains. While you
   probably think of Puerto Vallarta as a
   tropical beach destination, this location
   has other areas just waiting to be
   explored. Don't stop at the water; keep
   on going until you get to the mountains!
   The Sierra Madre Occidental is a
   mountain range that extends from the
   United States down into Mexico. An
   off-road vehicle tour is the best way to
   explore it. Tours in the area can be
   individually on an ATV or in a group
   with a dune buggy. The tours last for
   hours and most of that time is spent
   traveling through rugged trails straight
   up into the mountains. Our tour left
   from the middle of the city in Puerto
   Vallarta and we got to drive through
   back roads of the city and see what
   Puerto Vallarta is really like, not just the
   glittering touristy areas. It was stark and
   beautiful and heart-breaking with
   poverty unlike anything we've seen
   anywhere else. Our tour took us to a
   restaurant on top of a mountain with a
   layover that allowed us to eat some local
   fare, swim in the river, and do a tequila
   tasting. The guides were completely

focused on our safety, our comfort, and our fun. An amazing adventure! We used Wild Trek adventures and I highly recommend them. Wild Trek is located at Basilio Badillo #400 Col. Emiliano Zapata, Puerto Vallarta, Jalisco, Mexico. Phone is +52(322)222-8933. Or, toll free from the US at 1-800-493-9682. For more information, visit the website at www.wildtreksadventures.com.

The best way to see the beauty and ruggedness of the mountains. Wear old clothes because you'll be covered in dust.

3. **Go By Air:** <u>**Ziplining**</u> the **<u>tropical forest</u>**. The Sierra Madre Mountains is more of a tropical forest rather than a tropical jungle and the foliage and fauna

have to be seen to be believed. And, what better way to see it than climbing up high and zipping and flipping through the trees? The **Canopy El Eden** adventure is home to the most intense, most extreme zip lining I've ever done. Considering I've zip lined Fremont Street in Vegas and flung myself off the tallest zip line structure in America and North America, that's quite a statement. Canopy El Eden is the location where Arnold Schwarzenegger's movie *Predator* was filmed and you can walk in his footsteps and hike those same mountains. There are over 12 lines that criss-cross the site and hiking up the mountain is very strenuous, but the ride down is completely worth it. The guides seem to be more monkeys than men, zipping through the trees as if they were born to it and making it look so easy! When you're finished, end the day at **The Eden** restaurant sampling authentic Mexican fare and diving into the Mislamoya River, with a convenient rope swing leaving right from the restaurant. I highly recommend the guacamole and chips, made fresh while you swim! Phone from the United States is (888)558-3330. In Mexico, call +01(800)681-1858. For more

information, the website at
<u>www.canopytourspuertovallarta.com</u>.

You can't beat the view. You can't beat
the refreshments. You can't beat a rope
swing into cool water. You just can't beat
it!

4. **Go By Day or Go By Night.** While in
    Puerto Vallarta, you must take a trip to
    <u>Las Caletas</u>. By day, it is a tropical
    paradise and private beach. By night, it
    transforms into a Mayan fantasy called
    <u>Rhythms of the Night.</u> You can only

get to the location via a long boat ride by the tour group **Vallarta Adventures**, but every minute is worth it. As you pull up at the beach, you are greeted by costumed performers who lead you to the base of a temple/pyramid that is the scene for an incredible show. The performance showcases traditional dance and music. The costumes, the dancing-- it was all so amazing that I felt like a kid on Christmas morning with my mouth hanging open. The show ends right at dusk and you then wander down to the beach where tables are set up along the shore. An authentic Mexican buffet awaits you with plenty of 'American' food for those who might be tired of salsa and guacamole. There are as many courses as you want to eat and libations are poured liberally. When you're finished, you are free to walk around the beach. Each twist and turn of the trail is more amazing than the last and it seems but an instant until you hear the bells calling you back to the boat. A once in a lifetime experience! You'll get picked up outside Gate #9 at the Marina. In the United States, phone is (888)526-2238. In Mexico, call +52(322)226-8413. For more information, visit the website at

> **The amazing show (the stage is pictured above and took up the entire side of the mountain) would have been worth the long boat alone, but paired with a Mexican feast....this is a must do on your trip!**

5. **Act like a local.** Don't let your whole trip be taken up by fancy tours, though. Definitely make plans to spend a day or two exploring the wonders of downtown Puerto Vallarta at Malecón, a half-mile promenade overlooking the ocean. This central area has undergone a multi-million dollar expansion and is full of restaurants, shopping, and street performers and merchants selling authentic ware. The area also has some

amazing sculptures, 15 in total by
famous Mexican artists. The area is
heavily policed and well lit, so feel free
to stay past dark and walk around
enjoying the nightlife. If you're wanting
something more authentic, cross the
swinging bridge over the Cuale River
and shop in the local flea market, home
to unique gifts and friendly merchants.

All the action is at the Malecón, a half-mile wide strip downtown with American restaurants if you just can't stand chips and salsa for one more day.

6. **Act like a tourist**. One of the most
   recognizable landmarks in Puerto
   Vallarta is the Crown of Our Lady
   sculpture on top of the **Nuestra Señora**

de Guadalupe (Church of Our Lady of Guadalupe). The church itself is open to visitors. However, you won't get a tour here. Instead, you can go inside and spend a few moments in quiet worship, or, if you would like a full service, English services are given on Saturday and Sunday. The interior of the church is truly stunning and the square where it is located is full of locals. We

This local landmark dominates the city's skyline. Be sure to spend some time exploring its neighborhood.

were lucky enough to be there as a group was practicing for a dance competition and were treated to a free display with full Mexican costume! The square is hopping most days and nights and is located near quaint restaurants and shopping along cobble-stoned streets. The church is located at Hidalgo #370, Puerto Vallarta, Jalisco, Mexico. Phone is +52(322)222-1326.

Places To Eat

SeaFoodies will fall in love with Puerto Vallarta. There are a plethora of seafood restaurants with fresh catches from the sea. Naturally, their Mexican cuisine is outstanding. If none of the above eateries appealed to you, be sure to try these restaurants, some of the best places to eat in the area:

- It's definitely the best view in town. If you like seafood, you'll have to head inland at Puerto Vallarta. ***La Langosta Feliz* (The Happy Lobster)** has some amazing fresh fish and the best view of the tropical forest you will find. The entire restaurant is open air with no walls and sitting on the second floor feels just like you're eating in the treetops. The food was so good and they had the biggest prawns I have ever seen in my life. Everyone at the table got something different and it would be hard to say what was the best! What made the place so much fun though is that it was away from the usual tourist streets. It's on a little side street just outside of town and all the food was authentic. Most of the people there were locals. The Happy Lobster is located at

Rep. Dominicana 120 Altos, Lázara Cárdenas 4833, Puerto Vallarta, Jalisco, Mexico Phone is +52(322)223-1309. For more information, *en español*, check out the website at www.langostafeliz.com.

> **This mountain view at La Longosta dominates any ocean view we had.**

- Does recommending an Italian restaurant in Mexico seem odd to you? Me, too, and yet........the youngsters rebelled at eating Mexican cuisine for every meal. We decided to try **La Terrazza di Roma** for two other reasons: #1--its location. It is located in the Marina area right on the water. Watching the yachts and boats while eating on a pier overlooking the water was just too much fun. The open air pier had an air of romance about it. We were there for breakfast but I can imagine at night, with candlelight, it would be quite lovely. Reason #2--Well, the pier overlooking the water. This place was so much fun. While we were there, some locals followed an alligator underneath the pier. Alligators under our seats? Who knew they were even in Mexico? Maybe they were crocodiles, I don't know. And, the food? Quite good! No website, but for reservations or for questions, call (322) 221-0560.

If you don't care to sit on the water and open deck, there is also a more traditional eating area right across the street.

The restaurant is located at Puesta del Sol Club Tenis Marina Vallarta, Puerto Vallarta, Jalisco, Mexico.

- If you're hankering for some inexpensive, no frills, authentic Mexican, try **Tacos & Beer**. The name isn't very imaginative, but the food is truly delicious. And, when something is this good, why dress it up? My recommendations? The tacos and the beer, of course! They have a lot of hand-crafted beers to choose from and their tacos and homemade guacamole was some of the best we had while in Puerto Vallarta. Plus, it's convenient to the Marina and is a fun walk from the hotels in that area. Tacos & Beer is located at Paseo de la Marina, Marina Vallarta, Puerto Vallarta, Jalisco, Mexico. Phone is +52(322)209-0909.

Other Places of Interest

Unfortunately, it's just not always possible to visit EVERY great place. Here are some other options I just haven't gotten to yet:

- **Vallarta Jardin Botanico (Vallarta Botanical Gardens)**. This recently opened garden has a goal of collecting the most extensive display of Mexican orchids in the entire country. I would love to see this and their plant and floral displays. They have five tours, with one being complimentary. The tours focus on birds, "enchanted" waterfalls, and a hike into the nearby forest. The gardens are located at Carretera Puerto Vallarta a Barra de Navidad Km. 24, Las Juentas y Los Veranas, Cabo Corrientes, Jalisco, Mexico, 48447. International phone is +011+52(322)223-6182. Inside Mexico, phone is (322)223-6182. For more information, visit the website at www.vbgardens.org.
- **El Faro Lighthouse**. This 110-foot high lighthouse is actually a circular lounge that serves drinks overlooking the marina, complete with music. The bar is located at the Royal Pacific Yacht Club, Timón Paseo de la Marina 245,

Marina Vallarta. In Mexico, phone is (322)221-0542.

If you see or do something you think I should know about, please contact me at ccthomaswriter@gmail.com.

40800260R00019

Made in the USA
Lexington, KY
18 April 2015